Slave Song:

New Adventures With the Bell Witch

A genuine Southern ghost story
Of love and friendship,
Slavery and murder,
And one family's darkest
And best kept secret

By Kelly Stuard-Will
Co-authored with Timothy M. Will

Karitas Publishing
Salisbury, NC

I can remember the church on Long Street, the warm summer evenings, and the distant voice of the preacher. I am sleepily curled up on the front pew, and you are stroking my hair. The side door is open, so the evening breeze carries the green scent of the freshly mowed lawn, the earthy smell of the woods, and the sweet fragrance of honeysuckle vines.

If I peer from half-closed eyelids, I might see the occasional flash of a lightning bug or hear the cicadas in their night music...

-Good night, Daddy. Sleep well.

About the Artwork

When painting this cover, I chose to leave Katya's face blank. This is because every person who witnesses her is unable for some reason to form the words that actually describe her face, though they do tell me that she definitely has facial features. Her clothing is usually her gray dress and blue kerchief. The only exception is a formal black and white maid's outfit that one house guest is reported to have seen her in- the night that I was having a dinner party.

Special Note:

Because I wanted to make the finished manuscript an early "Father's Day Gift" and rushed through the writing, editing, and printing process, the first edition seemed "raw" and lacked a lot of the detail that this edition has. When my father died a week later, I was really glad that he got to see his legend put down on paper. However, to really appreciate our version of the ***Legend of the Bell Witch***, you need to understand me, my family, and the relationship dynamics behind this book. So, that's why we re-released it, as it is as much about us as it is about her.

Dear Reader,

What you are about to read is a true story, as accurate as we can tell it. We believe in truth, and in this case, the truth may make some people angry. It is a personal account of encounters with a historically famous ghost, one of the most famous ghosts in the American South.

This book is ***NOT*** *about Ouija boards, channeling, incantations or typical occult stuff. As my husband and I are Christians, we believe these practices are against God and put the soul in great danger. Instead our accounts are about simple communication, respect, justice and peace for the dead (albeit limited justice due to the fact that everyone involved is 2also dead.)*

You will also encounter concepts that you would not expect to find in a book on ghosts, many of them scientific in nature. As mystical as we are, together we, the authors, hold scientific degrees in biotechnology and electronics engineering, which involve employing knowledge of hardcore scientific principles in biology, genetics, recombinant DNA (genetic engineering), epidemiology, physics, organic chemistry and the structure of the atom.

Our world is not a simplistic one where spiritual or scientific exclusivism reigns supreme, but a complex place where these warring principles in pop culture often sit side by side in complete harmony or even blend into one another. We do not enjoy being classified or pigeon-holed and understand that God should never be placed in a box of limited human understanding. Believe it or not, many scientists and mystics secretly feel this way but remain silent, often for fear of exclusivists on both ends and society (as a whole) judging them unfairly.

To this day, the Bell Witch's legend inspires tremors of fear, but if you want to experience that, turn on the TV, go the library or cruise the Internet. You'll not be disappointed. You won't hear that much about historical accounts in this book. The specter of the Bell Witch already has many historians, and I feel that I would just be regurgitating the data that's already out there, much of it questionable at best.

Or you could rent the Hollywood travesty called, ***"An American Haunting,"*** *which apparently tried to say that the paranormal activities in Adams, Tennessee were caused by teenage angst and an incestuous relationship between Betsy Bell and her father. Yuck! John Bell was an ugly piece of work, but incest? "Hollyweird" has this habit of taking a popular tale and twisting it beyond recognition. Looking at the trailers, I didn't realize that they were speaking of the Bell Witch until I talked with my cousins from Tennessee. It just looked like the typical Hollywood drug trip fantasy. The folks in Adams were all scratching their heads, and in that, I had to join them.*

But, as this story officially begins in the early nineteenth century, you can guess that it's been embellished over the years; even specific dates are a bit fuzzy. (I looked up details for this book, and found that Lucy Bell, the mother in the Bell family, had supposedly married John as a preteen while he was in his early thirties. I know that child brides were popular, but I hope not that popular.

In July 2009, I went to Adams to find some sort of proof of what I'd experienced. Sadly, there was no mention of the legend my father, a native son of that community, had told me as a little girl. It was the usual party line. How could he, who grew up there, tell me something that the immediate Bell Family and their descendants would disavow? As Dad was very honest in nature, I can only believe that somehow the records of her true origin were altered, purged, or lost, if they had ever existed at all. For this was no poltergeist, no demonic being, but the ghost of a long dead African slave, who starved to death at the hands of John Bell.

Slavery has left an ugly mark on American history. People were treated as livestock. Families were often split up, their members sold and relocated to God-knows-where. It would have been fairly easy to kill a slave and wipe any trace of her away. We do have historical diaries and written accounts documenting the existence of slavery, but unfortunately, African-Americans were considered to have a percentage of the value placed on Caucasians. Even now, we're still finding lost slave graveyards and traces of a whole race, dehumanized and robbed of its dignity, self-respect, and self-worth.

Surprisingly, Kate has been seen and witnessed by a number of our friends and acquaintances over the years, and they all (having no way to compare notes with each other) describe her the same way. She is **always** *a large, middle-aged black woman, generally wearing a blue kerchief and a gray dress, the garb of a servant of the house.*

But the big difference is that the presence I know as the Bell Witch has actually been a kind, protective one. In fact, I do not call her "Kate," but "Katya," a name often given to a grandmother or elderly aunt. It is affectionate and denotes great respect.

Sadly, in 1996, my father had a triple stroke that altered his memories, and he lost the legend as he had taught it to me. Dad began to parrot the popular version because he had no recollection of the story that he had spoken about for years. It broke my heart. Strokes are infamous for changing personalities and losing or augmenting memories. My husband and I would try to remind him of what he had told us before, but it seemed as though the door to those remembrances was forever shut. I felt so alone because it was now squarely on my shoulders to remember and write down what I had always known from babyhood and give my father's legend new life in a book.

This is both her story and ours, and I feel that it is my duty to tell what I've experienced, before I get too old and my memory fades. I'm the heir and caretaker of what I believe to be the true legend, one that is anything but politically correct. It cannot die with me, but hopefully live on in these pages. If I can give some measure of peace and justice to someone enslaved, robbed of life, and maligned in death, then I do it willingly, with a loving heart.

Do you believe?

While most people are naturally fixated on the physical realm and cannot fathom what lies beyond it, ghosts are part of the spiritual fabric of every culture known to man. Despite the advances of science and the Information Age, the unexplained still captures our imagination. The paranormal is there to remind us that the universe is grander and more mysterious than we can imagine, and that this life is only a baby step into a greater adventure.

Believing often helps certain humans retain their youthful fire. When the eyes sparkle with the wonder of a child, the body will often reflect it. It's when the fire has gone out that we become jaded, cynical, and truly old. This is not about being naïve, but about accepting things we cannot explain. Nothing is sadder than to meet a human being who has lost that fire, particularly when they are young. It's as if the dreaming child has been crushed or driven out by the problems, stresses and strains of the world.

And believing is not about being mentally ill or schizophrenic. These are disturbing psychiatric disorders that often demand a lifetime of drugs with only management protocols, not cures. Those who've had paranormal experiences are often everyday people, with no history of mental disease or instability at all. They exude practicality, common sense, and live completely ordinary lives in other areas, with stable marriages and well-adjusted children.

Some scientists have reasoned that when someone with an incredible amount of life energy dies, that energy is released and disbursed into the ether of a home or geographical area. The Laws of Thermodynamics dictate that energy can be released but not destroyed. It simply changes form. And those who are sensitive to that life energy may see or experience it in some way.

An everyday example of powerful things we cannot see is the atom, that when split, releases an incredible amount of energy that can be harnessed to create electricity. But atomic energy is more famous for being the most destructive force ever unleashed by mankind upon the earth: leveling cities and towns; vaporizing animals and people; and leaving long-lasting, dangerous radiation that shortens lives through poisoning and diseases like cancer as well as causing mutations that result in horrific birth defects. No one can see an atom without an electron microscope, the most advanced microscope out there, but we definitely know it exists.

Speaking of measuring the unmeasureable, reputable paranormal investigators like TAPS (The Atlantic Paranormal Society) are employing scientific principles to rule out supposed "hauntings," so that what evidence is left can be scrutinized and quantified as true evidence of ghosts and inhuman manifestations via measuring temperature fluctuations, EVP (Electronic Voice Phenomena) where voices that cannot normally be heard are picked up through sensitive readings and recorded, and infrared photography, which measures levels of heat that comes from energy and living things. For every fake (and there are many of them) paranormal research is revealing things that are scary, thrilling, and defy the dogmatic exclusivism of mainstream science.

There's part of me that is very logical and rational. It respects the scientific world and is at home with machines, protocols, and test tubes. But ever since I was very small, I have always been aware of the spiritual realm. The existence of God, angels, demons and ghosts was and still is an integral part of my beliefs. My grandmother was gifted with the strange ability to draw spirits and to some degree, I have retained that gift. While she could see and speak with them, I can sense them. It's that feeling you get when you know you're being watched, as if turning your head suddenly, you might glimpse an unearthly face staring back at you. Walk into an empty room, and it seems full of activity, and people are still there, even though you cannot see them.

These are scary experiences to a child who wants an explanation for everything in life. We besiege our parents with a barrage of "whys" to questions they can barely answer and some that still leave them dumbfounded after decades. But my wise grandmother always said that our responsibility to the spiritual world lay in trying to make it more peaceful.

Besides prayer (our best weapon against spiritual assault) we were supposed help spirits with their unfinished business. Buried wealth should be found and put to proper use, and terrible wrongs must be acknowledged and put to right. Homes and areas with a dark past must be spiritually cleansed before people move in. It is always wise to bless a home by having a minster or priest to pray over where you will live. These actions are just and right by any religious standard, even a non-Christian one.

Always remember that mortal humans are not able to battle dangerous spiritual forces on their own, especially demons. I'm reminded of the TV series, ***Babylon 5***, where Captain Sheridan has to battle a Vorlon, a being of pure energy and immense power, but cannot truly do it without the help of Kosh, another Vorlon, and the First One called Lorien. So, a human had to enlist the help of other beings of pure energy and immense power.

Angels and their dark inverse, demons, are beings of pure energy, who can temporarily take a corporeal form if a situation calls for it. As humans, we cannot hope to battle them alone without the power of the One that created them behind us, often aided by great allies such as the Archangel St. Michael, the chief demon battler, my husband's patron saint.

Every so often, I run across the idea that Christians should never believe in ghosts. This flies in the face of scripture itself. In the Old Testament, we have the ghost of Samuel the prophet appearing before Saul on the eve of a battle. The Bible declares him dead, then goes on to describe the ghost's meeting with King Saul ***(1 Samuel 28:3-14, KJV)***. Was it wrong to have the Witch of Endor to conjure Samuel? Without a doubt, but the Bible declares that it was indeed Samuel and not a demon in disguise. And what would Samuel, a great prophet of God, be doing traipsing about after death? Saul is asked "which spirit?" denoting that there is more than one spirit out there to summon. Jesus speaks of the unforgivable sin of grieving the Holy Spirit, being ***neither forgiven in this life, nor the next***. ***(Matthew 12:31-32, KJV)*** The implication of those words is that there ***is*** a place where sins will be forgiven in the next life.

Christ had no trouble correcting the Jewish leaders on their faith but never spoke against prayer for the dead, which was (and still is) a palpable part of the Jewish faith today. Death was a common thing in that day. He would have seen his own relatives "sitting Shiva" and praying for the souls of their dead, but not a word? Remember, that Christ wanted us to share in Paradise; if this was a heretical practice, he would have certainly declared it so because the state of a human soul is of the highest importance to both Jews and Christians.

I discussed this in ***A Faraway Ancient Country,*** my first work, when I shared the Jewish prayer for the dead, the ***Eli Malei Rachamim***:

God of compassion,
Grant perfect peace in your sheltering Presence,
Among the holy and pure,
Who shine in the brightness of the firmament.
To the soul of our dear________,
Who has gone to his eternal rest.
God of compassion,
Remember all his worthy deeds in the land of the living.
May his soul be bound up in the bond of everlasting life.
May God be his inheritance.
May he rest in peace.
And let us answer: Amen. (Beliefnet.com 2/04/03)

One of the letters of St. Peter speaks of Jesus preaching to the "imprisoned spirits" between his death and resurrection. ***(1 Peter 3:18-20, 4:6, KJV)*** Why preach to them if there was no hope of redemption? There is no need for preaching in heaven, and hell is like a roach motel. (Thank you, "Raid" Roach Killer and Madison Avenue.) You can check in, but you can't check out.

St. Paul speaks of a man's deeds being burned away as if by fire until only the good ones survive- being cleansed. In Latin, the place of cleansing or purging of the last vestiges of one's sinful nature is called, "Purgatorio", or in modern English, "Purgatory."

The Apostle Paul also endorses the practice of prayer for the dead when he prays for his friend, Onesiphorus in his Second Letter to Timothy:

> The Lord give mercy unto the house of Onesiphorus; for he oft refreshed me, and was not ashamed of my chain: but when he was in Rome, he sought me out very diligently, and found me. ***The Lord grant unto him that he might find mercy of the Lord in that day: and in how many things he ministered unto me at Ephesus, thou knowest very well. (2 Timothy 1:16-18, KJV)***

If we analyze the way that Paul is speaking about Onesiphorus, he is talking about his friend in the past tense, in the same manner as the Jewish prayer mentioned before. Paul seems to separate the man, Onesiphorus, from the house of Onesiphorus. This is evidence that Onesiphorus is no longer living. The Apostle also asks for God's mercy on behalf of his friend, which hints that Paul does not believe that Onesiphorus died completely cleansed of his sins and their stains. But wouldn't this prayer be in vain if there is only heaven and hell, and no purgatory?

These are but a few of the passages found in both the Old and New Testaments, in the King James 1611 Bible. Now, you can see why Protestant Fundamentalists have such a problem with ghosts. Their very existence contradicts the belief that there is only heaven and hell. It's just easier to classify any spirit as a demon in disguise and be done with it. The Bible tells us to try the spirits to see if they're from God. But there would be no need to try the spirits if they were all demons in disguise.

So, spirits trapped in this middle state are on their way to heaven. The realm of spirits is a kind of spiritual "mud room" where they can clean up before entering into God's presence because he cannot abide with sin of any kind, no matter how trivial. Some of us enter that mudroom with a few grass stains and some mud on our shoes, while others barely get in the door, covered in muck to their eyeballs, and must do some serious cleaning before entering the throne room of the King of the Universe.

In Katya's case, I do believe that she was a human being. It's easy to see how grief, pain, prolonged hunger and thirst might have caused her to lose her mind. Ordinary people do this in the living state, so it isn't a big leap to understand that dying people may be doubly susceptible to it. It was her unjust enslavement and death that caused her to exact a terrible price from her killer and his daughter, a child determined to marry someone too much like her father. Our legal system understands the difference between being driven to kill after severe suffering versus cold-blooded murder, which is planned, usually for some type of gain.

As for the title "Witch," we must remember that, in the early 1800's, in the rural South, any paranormal phenomenon was branded as "witch." This includes places, peculiar lights and sounds, and ghosts.

Who are we?

While all of this activity comes from my father, according to my grandmother (who shared her genealogy), my mother's people were rooted in the Moravian Church (German Quakers) in the Piedmont of North Carolina. They may have had blacks as sharecroppers and general workers, but owning a human being was repugnant to them. Quakers have a long distinguished history of egalitarianism. Many hid and protected runaway slaves at great personal risk, being some of the most active abolitionists at the time.

Moravian history is rich in craftsmen and artisans, love of music, good food, and spirituality. To this day, one can experience life as a Moravian in Old Salem, NC. This fits, as most of the Yow family settled in Thomasville (not far from Old Salem), famed for its beautiful furniture. As for our immediate family, we're mainly Methodists and Independent Wesleyans, with a smattering of Baptists thrown in for good measure. Religion has always had a prominent place in both my father's and mother's families.

Personally, I am a native of Salisbury, North Carolina, which is approximately 40-45 miles north of Charlotte, and one of the oldest towns on the Eastern Seaboard (dating back to the late 1600's, but getting its official charter in the 1700's.) Unlike many places in the South, it was spared a fiery destruction when Sherman made his famous march to the sea, mainly due to the hospitality of one of its citizens. As a result, Salisbury was able to preserve its records as well as its historic houses and magnificent churches with their steeples and stained glass. In its heart, is the great old lady in her court of myrtle trees, a civil war memorial of an angel, holding a fallen soldier, with Valkyric overtones. Valkyrie were the choosers of the slain, the noble dead on the battlefield in ancient Norse mythology.

My home is also where you can find some of the best pork barbecue around. North Carolina is a barbecue mecca with the "Lexington Barbecue Festival" a few miles down the road. Traditionally, the meat does not swim in a thick sauce, but is lightly flavored with sweet red slaw and garnished with hush puppies (fried cornbread with tiny bits of onion). Sauce is generally served on the side as a condiment. Walking down the center of town, the nose is caressed with the rich smell of hickory and pecan fires and smoking meat. I grew up where great food is a natural standard, in a family where the ability to be a good cook is genetically encoded. I consider myself a pretty decent cook, though I have included Asian and Mediterranean food in my repertoire, specializing in Asian barbecue, roast lamb and a huge variety of New York styled cheesecakes in various shapes and flavors like: orange dreamsicle, lime daiquiri, mudslides with Kahlua liqueur and ribbons of fudge, cookies and cream, and amaretto.

I'm from a long line of fierce matriarchs. We've produced artists, reporters, nurses, CPAs, even missionaries and bootleggers- all great ladies and great mothers. No one ever sacrificed their principles or harmed their families to achieve great things beyond their home. Instead, they flourished in the modern world- balancing home with careers. As a child, I was encouraged to be independent, self-reliant, and to stand apart from the herd. Talents were always nurtured, and academic achievement was prized above social activities and sports.

You'd never know it to look at me, but I'm actually bi-racial. Like many Americans, I have American Indian or Amerind blood; my paternal grandmother was an Eastern Band Qualla Cherokee. People tend to see my fair skin and stop, but look closely and you'll also see that I have deep-set eyes, high cheek bones and a long, aquiline nose. My eldest sister keeps a perpetual tan that, combined with blond hair, has always given her a "Californian surfer" look. Blend this with English, Scottish, Irish, and German with just a hint of Mediterranean blood and you have my sisters and me. (One great grandmother had Spanish, Italian or Greek coloring with dark eyes, olive skin and black hair. She is reported to have made some of the best moonshine in her county, and was the mother of my maternal grandfather, an ordained Methodist minister.) I have always looked at my heritage and familial history as a kind of tapestry- woven with many colors, textures and dimensions. Take one away, and I wouldn't be the person that I am. Every element contributes.

Generally speaking, when most people think of being bi-racial, they see only mixes of African and Caucasian people. Actually, the label "bi-racial" can also apply to Amer-Asian and Amer-Indian, Latin and Polynesian peoples of mixed race. Perhaps, I should stop for a second and talk about being Amer-Indian. Children with a bi-racial heritage are often forced to choose one race over another when they should be able to appreciate both sides of their heritage. This is what happened to me.

My maternal grandmother was generally very egalitarian in her business life, often selling to blacks when other vendors would not. She sold "Raleigh's" products (a kind of cross between Amway and Avon) and ran a route throughout the civil rights era in which most of her clientele were African-American. But, she, like so many of her time, entertained racist views. So, it was more than a little upsetting when her only daughter married a half-Amerind son of a sharecropper. (She had always wanted Mom to marry a doctor or lawyer or professor- someone in the social elite. This was also a big problem in her eyes.)

As she raised me while my parents worked, I had to deal with my grandmother's hatred of my father on a daily basis. We had terrible fights, and I couldn't imagine my dad as a half-breed. He just had smoldering good looks. Of course, my Dad took her rejection hard, was deeply resentful, and rightfully so, as he was hardworking, very religious, and deeply devoted to his wife and family.

I became a battle ground with each wanting me to reject the other. For a little while, I parroted my grandmother's beliefs, but then I began to make so many friends from so many places.

By the time I was a teen, that sort of thing had no real place in my life. And one day, I finally realized that I was mix of two races- neither completely white nor Amerind. And being caught between them, I fiercely loved both my grandmother and father, and each had a specific place in my heart despite their flaws.

Ironically, I'm a mixture of these two family antagonists, hopefully in their best forms. I have my father's sense of humor, gregarious nature, and ease around people, but I also have my grandmother's resourcefulness, talents, love of knowledge, and no-nonsense, sometimes blunt, nature. I've also inherited my dad's spirituality and respect for the natural world coupled with my grandmother's mystical nature.

I would have loved to have known my Amerind grandmother, but she died when my father was still a child himself. The closest that I ever got to her was when I visited the Cherokee Reservation in the western mountains of North Carolina. I was privileged to attend one of the oldest outdoor dramas in the US, ***"Unto These Hills."*** The play tells the story behind the ***Trail of Tears***, one of the worst atrocities perpetrated on the Amerind peoples in America, made even more egregious because the Cherokee were extremely cooperative, peaceful, and had adapted to the English language and the Christian faith.

I was overcome with emotion and cried when I heard the Amerind singers sing hymns that I had grown up with as a child in their native tongue, especially the old spiritual, "***At the Cross.***" I felt like my Indian grandmother and father were sitting close beside me, and there was an unbelievable feeling of unity, pride and love. I knew that they were there, and they were pleased.

In the world of being politically correct, many American Indians bristle at the label of "Native American," seeing every native born American as a "Native American." Instead, they usually prefer their tribal autonym, the name that they call themselves. Official names are also often what their enemies actually called them. But most are okay with 'American Indian" or "Amerind," which I like. The name "Cherokee" is actually an Anglicization of "***Tsalagi,***" which means the "The Principle People." In fact, Amerind tribes collectively see themselves as "The People."

As for the concept of race, from a scientific position, it is foolish to believe that one race is better than another as humans have few differences on the inside. Differences in coloring, bone configuration, hair texture, etc. are our species' natural adaption to differing environments. Colder climates demanded lighter skin tones in order to get Vitamin D from the sun, while darker pigments developed to protect from the harshness of solar rays that struck around the middle of the planet. Smaller nostrils developed in cold climates in order to keep freezing air from damaging lungs, while heat from warmer areas demanded wider nostrils to facilitate better breathing. Even fat deposits were shaped from varying climates. Colder-climated humans needed to insulate their internal organs while those in hotter areas stored their fat reserves on their hips and buttocks in order to keep internal organs from overheating.

So, all the outward characteristics that we see as "races," are really very strong evidence of natural selection. Traits developed because those who survived specific climes passed their physical traits, while those who did not, did not pass their genetic information to a new generation. Sociologically, each specific race or culture has its own strengths and weaknesses. There are concepts that are great to emulate and problems that should be avoided. Being wise to why people look differently and understanding their culture are important elements that help us to reject familiar and destructive behavioral patterns that seek to classify and prejudge. (Now you see what it means to be both mystical and logical.)

Socially, for all intents and purposes, I was an "only child." Both of my older siblings are more like cousins than sisters, having grown up in an earlier generation. They were blond, super-achieving social butterflies, and I was (and still am) the rebel of the family- a creative, eccentric storm queen who disappeared into books and led a somewhat secretive life. In many ways, I have always been separated from my sisters, and when our parents died, this separation was more pronounced.

Though naturally outgoing, friendly, and talkative, I was raised primarily by my grandmother to the point of spending the week with her and the weekend with my parents. This added to the rift between my parents and me, as I often talked and acted like her. Most people identify with their same sex parent, but Nana was my principal caregiver. My sisters were closer to my parents. I often felt (and still do feel) like an afterthought. After all, the family was well-established when I came along. Now that our parents have passed, we hardly ever speak to one another, and I still mourn the loss of my family and long for a closeness between my sisters and I that truly never existed.

My Catholic conversion completely solidified my estrangement from my family. I only ever truly wanted their understanding and respect for the spiritual path that I had chosen. It breaks my heart that I can never share **Midnight Mass** at Christmas and the glorious **Triduum** at Easter with relatives that I believe to have developed a misshaped view of my faith. The beauty and biblical relevance of those experiences transcends denominational boundaries and unites people when minds and hearts are open. Neither of these celebrations would have interfered with their church and family obligations but would've added new depth and richness to their own holiday experiences. And while Tim and I tried to share in my family's celebrations and traditions, I do not feel that our efforts were ever reciprocated, except on two specific occasions, our 10th and 25th Anniversary Renewal of Vows.

This deeply grieves me, but I would not sacrifice my faith or the person I am- simply for approval. Being independent and apart has become a badge of honor, earned from rejection and tears. If they ever accept me, it will have to be as I am. My sisters and I have never shared friends or moved in the same social circles. I suppose that I never liked being in their shadow and sought to create my own distinct world and circle of friends.

Growing up in the '70s and '80s, I spent my summers at the local YMCA, where I learned how to swim and acquired all sorts of friends from every culture, race, or group imaginable. I've also dated people from other cultures and religions. My first boyfriend was a Muslim from Afghanistan. (He was an extremely handsome, intelligent and charming man.) The second guy was an Orthodox Jew who bore a striking resemblance to Tom Baker of ***Doctor Who*** fame.

Then, I met and married this Catholic boy from a good family who was the son of a retired Air Force major. Timothy Michael Will is a blend of Scottish, English, German, and Nordic nationalities with Semitic blood. His great grandmother was Jewish. It's weird but he'll get that "question mark" inflection in his voice that many Jews have been famous for, a kind of cultural inheritance that his mother often has. Our wedding anniversary is also the day on which we were both born.

Tim grew up in a boisterous clan of nine children- five boys and four girls. Most of these siblings (eight out of nine) are college educated- many of which have had federal, state, and municipal jobs. According to the last count, I am aunt to 19 regular and 14 grand nephews and nieces and take great pleasure and pride in their achievements and productive lives.

Originally raised Catholic, most of the Will children have chosen their own spiritual paths. Sadly, Tim remains the only child still active in the Catholic faith, but over the years, he has created a rich spiritual legacy with godchildren in the faith and numerous unofficial lost puppies. I was his first student and celebrated the 20th Anniversary of my conversion in 2012.

Now that I am officially middle-aged, I have determined to change my life for the better, being basically a homemaker for over 26 yrs., with jobs that made "butter and egg" money. College takes up the bulk of my time as I have a post-graduate schedule and a career in health promotion in my sights. My husband, who was permanently disabled in 2006, is currently working toward a Master's degree as well, majoring in conflict resolution, a specialized area in psychology.

For both of us, writing is a great passion. We still love books and are fascinated by archeology/anthropology, history, world culture/religion, folklore, mythology, music, art, dance, crafts, and great food. We follow current events and pop culture, having developed tastes in science fiction/fantasy and Japanese Anime, which covers a wide selection of genres much like normal movies and TV shows. We recycle, share our home with rescued animals (and the occasional lost human puppy,) and currently workout 6 days a week at the local YMCA

One of my mentors (an Anglican priest of blessed memory) often declared us to be "Christian Hippies," reminiscent of the early twentieth century bohemians in Paris because we had no problems discussing hot issues and difficult subjects, all garnished with food, music, and wild, often playful, conversation. You could say that I'm unusual for a native born North Carolinian. But despite all these differences, I'm still an old country girl at heart, loving my parents and treasuring my father's stories. Maybe that was what drew Katya to me in the first place.

Left Alone to Tell the Tale

"Daddy's dead." Those final words just thundered in my head. It was 10:30 pm on June 11, 2010 when my eldest sister called to say what I had known all along. Walter G. Stuard had gone to Presbyterian Hospital in Charlotte, NC for open heart surgery on a valve. He went to sleep and didn't wake.

His pre-op had been at 5am. Hours and hours later, there was no word of recovery. Good news in the operating room is usually quicker. But the longer things take, the scarier it gets. I had every right to be worried. We knew that the prognosis was grim, but there had still been the hope that he'd come storming through. After all, my father had survived a triple stroke, diabetes, Alzheimer's, and asbestosis. After two bouts of cancer and chemotherapy, he still had his thick, silver-white hair, which is rare for cancer patients. (Hair loss is almost a "given" where chemotherapy is concerned.) Put simply, Dad had the constitution of an ox. It's odd that his heart would get him after so many brushes with death.

In his late 70's, Walter ("Jack") was still pretty active, puttering around town, visiting our mother, who could no longer walk and lived at a nearby nursing home, and taking care of Maddie, his black dachshund. We used to joke that Dad would outlive us all. (I did want to warn people that he was on the road and say, "Ya'll be careful, now!")

Most people aren't allowed foreknowledge of their death, but I do believe that God blessed my father with such a foreshadowing. He seemed determined to put his estate in order, spend a lot time with his minister packing those spiritual bags, even making arrangements with us to care for his dog. The day before he passed, he spent the day with our mother, his wife for almost fifty-five years. Then, he drifted away into eternity. It was an abrupt, but peaceful end to fruitful life that boasted three daughters, four grandsons, and numerous friends.

So many people were shocked with his death. Jack Stuard exuded an old country boy's charm and a sense of humor. He was famous for off-hand remarks like, ***"Hey, what's on your mind besides your hair?"*** or if he thought something had all the extras, he'd exclaim, ***"That thing's got streetlights and running water."*** People would ask, *"How are you, today?"* and he'd smile and answer, ***"I'm present."*** Or declare, ***"I've been better, but it cost more."*** How could someone so full of life be dead?

He knew people from every corner in the community. Daddy could walk in a grocery store for bread and milk and stay for a half-hour talking to friends. I have my father's gift of gab, and do the same thing. It's really weird for my husband when he's at the grocery store and a stranger comes up and tells him to say hello. We've out of town and I'll bump into folks I've known at some period of my life. It's a good thing that Tim isn't a possessive man or he'd have had a nervous breakdown a long time ago.

To this day, people still come up and say that they're sorry to hear about my folks, which is always strangely comforting, as if the whole community mourned our loss. At the funeral, I was amazed that three congregations were represented and relatives came from two other states. There were even attendees from my mother's nursing home. CNAs, housekeepers, nurses, and administrators were there to share in the laughter and tears, though my mother was technically their patient. I kept telling them all not to hug me because as soon as one did, I'd cry.

Why write down these memories? I simply wish that my readers could have known my father. He was a good man who spent most of his existence devoted to his faith, his family and his friends. He was deeply honest, never drank alcohol or smoked, and he rarely swore. Looking back, I realize how blessed I was to be raised by such a father when so many others don't have that heritage.

Society wants to make the sexes interchangeable with no innate value of their own, while sociologists and psychologists keep tracing evils such as promiscuity, violence, and drug abuse to parental roles. A father's effect on his daughter is often subtler than a mother's because they are usually secondary caregivers. But a man who actively values his daughter is less likely to see her in a destructive lifestyle later in life. Men also teach their sons how to behave in a marriage and be fathers.

We celebrate love and marriage but always assume that nothing ever truly lasts. To say that my parents were married for over 50 yrs. gets a lot of raised eyebrows today along with a healthy amount of amazement and admiration. My mother never recovered from my father's death. A little over a year later, Reba Stuard passed beyond the veil herself. Mom hardly ate or drank, hastening her departure from this life, dying mainly of grief and loss.

In the end, Mother was more lucid and clear-headed after months of dementia and completely losing touch with the real world. She recognized family and friends and knew who was visiting her. Isn't it odd that this often happens when we die? But with lucidity, came a common refrain among the dying.

The nursing staff reported that she would have long, ongoing conversations with Daddy. Once, a nursing assistant and family friend reported that when she tried to feed Mom, my mother kept insisting that she give some food to Jack. (He'd been waiting out in the hall the whole day.) Early in the following morning, my mother passed away. This so reminded me of watching an old black and white version of ***Wuthering Heights***, when the lovers are reunited in death.

I truly believe that we see our loved ones before death; they come back to comfort us and bring us peace in our passing. Mom was drifting back and forth from the living world and the spiritual one. My father could sense her crossing over and came to help her do just that. Though Dad's death was a shock, I was ready to let my mother go- after seeing her suffer so much. I prayed to God for her release. My biggest regret is that I didn't tell Mom, ***"You know Mama, you can go on now. Don't worry about me. I'm OK. See you on the other side."***

Was I sad to see them go? Yes. You don't feel your age until your parents die. There's a part of all humans that longs to stay a child and enjoy life while the adults sort everything out. When you lose your parents, you are reminded that the safety net is gone, and you have to be the adult and must sort things out yourself.

Daddy's Legacy

Ever since I could remember, I have always known about the Bell Witch. I heard snatches of the legend on long, sultry nights, when there was nothing on TV, and our Tennessee cousins were in town. I would play in the backyard, hearing the crackle of a campfire with its aromatic smells, and seeing the flash of lightning bugs. It was a tale meant to be shared in the evening, when the dishes were washed and put away and the adults were settling down to talk of family and life back in Dad's hometown of Adams, Tennessee.

In that day, you might have four channels on TV- five or six, if you had VHF/UHF channels. Your remote control was one of your children, who would sometimes hold the "rabbit ears" for better signal reception if the weather was bad. Only wealthy people could afford cable, and the Internet was unheard of. So, we had to keep ourselves entertained and learn actual social skills- something that is sorely lacking today in a society that cannot be separated from cell phones or computers.

My father, being half-Native American, would take on the guise of a shaman or venerable chief as he spoke, his dark eyes glinting in the firelight. There was a solemnity, an assurance that he was speaking the truth, and I was drinking in every word. It wasn't just entertainment to me. He was speaking of real events.

When I was six, our family moved out of our house in the city to a three bedroom mobile home in the country. This was mainly due to the fact that my grandmother's relationship with my Dad, which was never good, had reached a boiling point. Our home was just too close for comfort, being less than a block away.

So, we moved. The country was a harsh change from the beauty of our little street with its magnificent oaks and lush flowers. One of the few consolations was the blackberry bushes, growing wild in the backyard, which I truly enjoyed and regularly feasted on.

Now, we were on newly developed land, in a fresh-from-the-factory home. Imagine how my parents felt when they began to hear footsteps, pacing up and down the hall toward the back bedrooms (mine and theirs). Somehow, we had managed to get our own supernatural security guard. No one was attacked or harmed in any way, but this always seemed to go on at night.

Being both unnerved and unrested, my father (the devout man that he was) called for the elders in our little Wesleyan church to come and "plead the Blood of Jesus" to send whoever it was away. He felt that we had a "haint," possibly the Bell Witch, and had no wish to interact with it, even if it was a good spirit intent on protecting us. Dad was simply too terrified to deal with the spectral world.

Though the nightly patrols had ended, the presence remained with us. There were times that I felt that I might just see her out of the corner of my eye one day. Like I've said, it was that feeling that there was someone in the room when the normal senses said, "no."

"Daddy, could you tell me about the 'Legend of the Bell Witch?'"

Looking back, I believe those words cemented my connection to Katya. I had always known that the Bell Witch was a famous specter. There are books on her in the Library of Congress. Even now, Katya's a popular subject for TV shows. (We'll get to her hijinks when we watch these shows later.) But the Bell Witch that my father spoke of was not same ghost from popular Tennessee folklore.

After years of listening to snatches of conversation of my father's stories, this was the first time I had demonstrated any particular interest in the legend. (She'd probably been waiting very patiently for a sign.) But then again I was thirteen now, the perfect age where kids start really developing into young adults. This was not just a casual question, but the fruition of serious thought and deliberation. I had always loved ghost stories; they were like candy to me. I would inhale volumes of them at the local library, and I was gifted with a taste for legends and folklore that my sisters, with all their beauty, wit, and charm had never shown (too practical, I guess.) Even so, I had never had the courage to ask until now.

My father was driving at the time, and the atmosphere in the car seemed to thicken with anticipation and his sobering thoughts. This man always had the demeanor of an old troubadour, an ancient bard. Dad cleared his throat and began to speak,

"In 1782, John Bell married Lucy Wilson from Edgecombe County, North Carolina. She was from a wealthy family, and part of her dowry was a slave named Kate. Lucy and Kate were very close, having been raised together. Though legally mistress and slave, these two were the best of friends, like sisters. Lucy relied on Kate's counsel when running the house and dealing with the other servants.

"John Bell, like typical men of that time, saw women, in general, as property, with no rights, to be seen and never heard. Race didn't really matter. Women were stupid, and meant to be shepherded- never empowered. He never treated his wife like a distinct person apart from himself. Instead, he viewed her as an

extension of himself with no personality, hopes, and dreams that were her own.

"But Lucy and Kate made a formidable combination. Normally, Lucy was a very mild lady and could be bent to his will, but Kate gave her courage. John grew to despise everything about their friendship and wanted desperately to rid himself of this troublesome slave. The problem was that Kate was a dower slave and the strict property of Lucy, and John knew that his wife would never sell or barter away someone whom she saw more as sister and friend.

"So, John contrived to provoke Kate enough to lay hands on her, to override his wife's authority as Kate's mistress, and make Kate submit to his authority alone. He goaded, pushed, and prodded, until the woman was at her breaking point, and being so, she threatened him, which was all that John needed.

"Still afraid of dealing too harshly with her, John locked Kate up in a corn crib, hoping for a more docile slave after she apologized for her words. It didn't work. Kate refused to give in and take back her words, and hours turned into days as the slave slowly starved to death. She gnawed the flesh from her hands to stay alive. With her last dying breath, she cursed the man who had left her to a long, lingering death and swore vengeance on him and anyone like him in the family.

"While Lucy was deeply grieved at the loss of her dearest friend, John was determined to put it all behind him, thinking all the aggravation was over. He couldn't have been more wrong.

"A few days later, someone saw a large, menacing black cat in the fields. As this was obviously a wild animal, there was a thorough search of the property. Nothing could be found. Next, another person witnessed an old black man, sitting in a rocking

chair, in the middle of a field. Calling to him didn't a get a response. The man just sat, peacefully rocking in his chair- not answering any threat to leave. So, a party of men was assembled, and coming back to the area, found nothing again.

"From that moment, the specter of the Bell Witch became a grim reality. She slammed doors and windows, pulled covers from sleeping occupants and played a variety of pranks, mostly aimed at those who were hateful to her in life- the lion's share of attention being aimed at John Bell.

"In the end, Kate succeeded in killing her oppressor. John Bell became ill and was given a medicine to take by the local doctor in town. At first, he seemed to get better then took a turn for the worst. When the doctor checked with his patient, he found the medicine had been changed.

"Wondering about its effects, the doctor gave it to a house cat. The animal howled in misery and died in front of them. The poison was a powerful unknown substance that caused John Bell to nasty away from the inside out. There was nothing to be done.

"The funeral might have been a peaceful one, but the Witch laughed and catcalled through the whole thing, declaring that John Bell was burning in hell. Shocked mourners were unnerved at her complete lack of respect.

"Next to John, the Bell Witch centered her attention on young Betsy Bell, who was like her father and had taken up with a young man, Joshua Gardner that the ghost did not approve of."

Let me stop the story for just a second and explain ***why*** I believe the ghost did not want Joshua Gardner as a future mate to Betsy Bell. This is a common refrain in psychology and sociology. As stated earlier, men and women used their parent of the opposite sex as a template on which to choose a mate.

Parents model how to behave in future life- even what to look for in a mate. This is why dysfunctional and destructive behavior in families is so pervasive.

A husband or wife may seem a world away from a person's mother or father, but there can be the smallest trace of that parent in the new mate. My father is a very religious man, with a strong sense of family. This I saw in my husband, even though both men are very different.

Dad was a yellow dog democrat. (If a yellow dog ran on the democratic ticket, he'd have voted for it.) Tim tends to be conservative; voting on a candidate based on his/her personal voting record and how closely it resembles our values. If you don't have what it takes, he really doesn't care about anything else- religion, ethnicity, race, or culture. So, you can guess that there was a moratorium on political discussions around my father.

But what if a young woman's father were demanding, controlling, belittling- treating the opposite sex as property with no voice, no rights of any kind? She may be unwillingly drawn to a man like that because it was all she knew as a child. It was how her father had treated her mother, and in some twisted way, this was normal in her eyes. This is why domestic violence and drug/alcohol abuse runs in cycles in families. It is programmed into our psyches from an early age.

My father continued on:

"Betsy Bell was determined to marry Joshua Gardner, and no ghost was going to change that. So, she disappeared from her home one day, off to see a preacher with her love. When the Witch caught up with them, they were both whipped back home

like wayward children. After that Joshua Gardner relinquished the object of his affection. Betsy Bell was left alone- once she turned her attention elsewhere. But Kate still loved her mistress, even beyond the grave. Lucy took ill with scurvy, a deficiency in Vitamin C that killed many people in that day. Remember, there was no refrigeration or mass transit, so getting citrus fruit was impossible.

"The doctor declared that without getting certain foods like lemons, limes, or oranges, Lucy would die. The next day, a large bowl of citrus fruit was found next to Lucy's bed. Other accounts have the spirit singing to her mistress as she recovered from her ordeal. And Lucy did make a full recovery due to the kindness of the spirit.

"It was in 1839 that Kate told the family that she was going away for 100 years, but that she would appear to all future generations of the Bells after that. In 1939, the old farm became the scene of new paranormal activities. Once again, the black cat was seen, menacing in the fields. Then, someone saw the old black man sitting in his rocker. One member of the community walked into his kitchen one morning and found mounds of popped popcorn lying everywhere with no possible reason for being there. She was back."

I stared back at my dad and asked, ***"Has anyone ever seen her? What does she look like?"*** Dad replied, ***"She's a large black lady, with a gray dress and blue kerchief on her head."***

First Contact

In the moonlit night,
The farmhouse is sleeping.
She drifts past the quiet chicken coup.
The peacock sentinel looks on without a sound.
The family dog cocks his head in wonder.
And the still house of those artist cousins
Welcomes a silent visitor and whispers,
"Why, she's right in there.
Hear her heart beat?
It sings to you."

Visiting my cousins in Tennessee is a favorite memory of mine. The Cooks were decidedly different from the rest of my family, free-spirited, with an easy charm and a healthy sense of humor. They were a family of artists- brimming with liberal thought and pop culture.

The patriarch of this family is Marian Cook, a very talented still-life painter who still has a studio in Goodlettsville, TN. His eldest son, Barry, went on to work for Disney for over twenty years, his biggest project being the movie, ***Mulan,*** based on an actual legend. (My cousin went to mainland China to research it.) Both men lived and studied in Paris, perfecting their artistry there. Other members of this family have careers in commercial art and cartooning as well classical art. Mandy Cook was nice enough to paint the book cover of ***A Faraway Ancient Country,*** my first book.

The matriarch of this family is called Stella whom we call "Stella Belle." This amazing woman raised five children before traipsing off to Africa to serve with a group of other women as a Baptist missionary in Upper Volta during the Ethiopian famine of the 1980's. Then, she served in Central America in that capacity as well- all while leaving Papa to man the fort at home. After that, she attended college and completed her education. She is a wonderful example of a full life with a vibrant faith and loving family, the archetype that I was raised with. Stella's technically a cousin, but is more like a sister to my father as they were basically raised together. He had lost his own mother at the age of nine, and was kind of adopted by Stella's mother, so I tend to view Stella as an aunt.

I've said before that "la Maison Cook" was a cross between Pipi Longstocking's house and Frankenstein's lab- a treasure trove for an inquisitive child. The Cooks were never short on the odd or wacky: artwork everywhere, antiques, books, a pool table, bird cages filled with parakeets and a profusion of animals from the typical dogs and cats, to goats, and chickens to a large flock of peacocks that ran around, leaving brilliant blue-green feathers everywhere. Peacocks were the best burglar alarms, making a terrible racket when you drove up.

Perhaps the oddest thing that I ever saw was an actual human skeleton, crumpled up in a corner in the entrance hall. It had probably been "liberated" from some science lab at the local high school. And I knew it was real because of the discolorations on the bones. Plastic skeletons usually have a flat cream color with little definition to the nuances left by scars and wear and tear activities such as sports or repetitive work. This one had all the marks of once being the physical home of a living soul.

It was in this house, in Goodlettsville, a short distance from Adams, that I had my first solitary experience with the Bell Witch, the ghost my father called "Old Kate." My parents and I were visiting in the summer of 1982 when I was 16, give or take a month, and I elected to stay in the den because it was much cooler than the stifling heat of the upstairs bedrooms. So, I pitched my sleeping bag there and slowly drifted off to sleep, breathing in the aroma of warmed, hardwood floors and antiques.

It must have been around 2 or 3 am when I awoke suddenly, for no reason. No noises, midnight thirst, hunger or need for the bathroom to speak of, just a rustic room bathed in silvery light streaming through the curtains. It all seemed peaceful with no visible changes. Artwork, antiques, and pool table were all present and undisturbed. But the room had become heavy with a palpable presence near my favorite spot, the large flagstone fireplace which dominated this family room. So, there it stood, witnessing the rise and fall of deep sleep.

I was no longer a tiny infant, or a wild child of six or seven, but a plump young woman lost in my secret teenage world. I turned my head toward the fireplace and sniffed the air like a rabbit sensing danger and excitement. My normal eyes said that the room was empty, but that part of me that sensed the spectral world felt the gaze of supernatural eyes.

A simple thought came into my head. It said not to be afraid, that it was Kate, and to tell her I was OK. So, I sat up and spoke aloud to the night, to the spirit that I knew was there, ***"I'm okay, Kate. I'm fine. Don't you worry 'bout me."***

In the blink of an eye, the room was truly empty, and I was alone again. Laying back down, fluffing my pillow, I closed my eyes again and drifted back into teenage dreams. I had always heard about how fierce and scary this ghost was, and yet through my initial fear, I felt that this idea was all wrong. Instead, there was a feeling that she was a guardian, a protective presence, a kind of ghostly grandma. We seemed kindred to one another.

From that point, I sensed her presence. Sometimes, she would let me know that it wasn't all a dream, by moving or knocking small things over, like the small vanity lamp on my antique Ginny Lynn dresser, an inheritance from my grandmother. (I love that old thing. It's still beautiful with its round mirror and warm reddish brown finish.) Then, there were the stuffed animals that hung from the ceiling. Even when there was no hint of a breeze in the room, Katya would make them spin. I'd always speak aloud, and say, ***"OK, I know you're here, but could you just stop for a minute? It's getting weird."***

My grandmother, for all her strict Christianity, was also a mystic. As a child, she taught me to verbally acknowledge ghosts, remembering that they were still people though incorporeal. Speaking aloud and treating them as human beings were important steps in maintaining the peace within a house. Imagine being without a voice and unable to affect the world around you like you once did, and the sheer force of will is the only thing that allows you to move objects or communicate with others, simple things that the living take for granted.

Dante was right!

Tim's Memories

Before I began this chapter, let me tell our readers that my life is 99.99% normal. I've worked most of my life in blue-collar jobs such as maintenance and machinery positions. I love my family and am devoted to my marriage and my faith. I enjoy doing Sudoku and will often play mathematic games with license plates when driving around.

I don't see a ghost behind every tree and understand that the unknown is not a catch all. In fact, I'm a huge fan of the ***Ghost Hunters*** TV show on the Syfy channel that always tries to disprove the paranormal and is very hesitant to label anything as "haunted." However, there is always that .01% of my life that defies logic and reminds me that I don't have all the answers.

Most people assume that you cannot be both spiritual and scientific. Most people are wrong. I guess you could say that I'm a combination of logic, science, and math coupled with a healthy respect for that which cannot be quantified- a kind of mystical Mr. Wizard. My father was the same way, having a number of engineering degrees from respected universities. Kenneth John Will had once thought of being a Catholic priest but decided on family life, military service, and a career as a civil engineer with the Florida Department of Transportation. So, the world that I hail from is a curious blend of what most people classify as opposing elements.

My first encounter with ghosts was when I was a small boy living in an old plantation styled home in Monticello, FL that had once been the property of a prominent man in the community, Judge Byrd. One night, I woke up to see a ghostly gentleman pass through my bedroom- to a door that had been painted shut years ago- and beyond it. Needless to say, I spent the rest of the night under the covers, afraid to move. The next morning, I carefully examined the door to find that it was still painted shut and would not open no matter how hard I tried. That was my only encounter with spirits until I met Kelly, but not my only experience with the unknown.

Nine years before I met my wife, I dreamed an odd dream of my wedding. It was held in a church that I was unfamiliar with and officiated by a priest that I barely knew. But the weirdest part was the fact that I was the altar boy at my own wedding and that I escorted the bride down the aisle. When I married my wife, it was not under those strange circumstances. We had been married by an assistant clerk of the court in Quincy, Florida, and no detail matched.

However, on the first anniversary of the marriage, we had the union blessed by a priest that I only knew in passing, who had been a spiritual mentor of my wife in a church we have never been in before. My wife knew how important my faith was to me and my parents and that not having the union blessed was placing me at a distance from my faith as I could not legitimately partake in the sacraments, so she sat about arranging the ceremony with a personal friend and mentor who had been her first contact with Catholicism.

It was a private affair with just us, the priest, and a close family friend as a witness. As the priest explained his vestments to our witness, he casually asked me to go and light the candles, knowing that I had been an altar boy in my youth, which I did. Then, I came back and escorted my wife down the aisle to the altar. It wasn't until we were driving back when I realized that this day had been literally dreamed about, nine years earlier, long before I met my wife. It would take years before I would realize that, in this dream, I already was married, at least civilly, because I had escorted her down the aisle, and her father had not "given her away."

My wife Kelly Stuard stole my heart the first time that I saw her. She had eyes that you could drown in and a smile that lit up the room. Intelligent, hard-working, playful and creative with a strong religious streak, this girl was like me, a mingling of academics and spirituality. People find it interesting that we were born on the same day- exactly four years apart. But I've always joked that God gave me a birthday present when I was four years old; it just took another nineteen years to meet her.

Now, I had read stories about the Bell Witch, but had no idea that I was about to walk into this ghost story. When Kelly told me about Kate, I was moving her down to Florida. We were on US-319 between Thomasville, GA and Tallahassee. The car had no air conditioning, so we had the windows down. The night air was heavy with moisture, as only a June evening in the Deep South can be. And as she spoke I got the feeling that there was someone in the car with us, quietly watching.

The night grew darker and deeper with each word, and I was drifting out of the 20th century into the distant past- a place that whispered treachery and murder. It's easy to say that the whole experience was atmosphere and suggestion, but this was just a tiny step in a big adventure into the unknown. A few months later, I would see Kate and interact with this legendary ghost on an unimaginable level.

We moved into an old cinderblock, stucco apartment in the student slums of FSU. Florida is filled with these buildings- no insulation (scorching in the summer, cold and damp in the winter) with mud brown tiled floors and windows any burglar would love. The oddest thing was the wall around the front porch, which you stepped up and then down into- to prevent flooding when it rained.

Our place wasn't much, but it was what we could afford. Like many young couples, our date nights included trips to the dollar movies. It was a cheap, fun escape, and the movies were usually fresh from first-run movie houses. That evening, we were seeing an old Mark Harmon film called ***Summer School***, so this movie was a comedy.

Unfortunately, the writers and producers of the movie did a bloody homage to the ***Texas Chainsaw Massacre*** in which a group of teens recreated a scene to freak their substitute teacher out. Even in the movie, it was faked, but because it was so graphic, bloody and completely unplanned for, I couldn't seem to let go of the mental image. So, I went to bed that evening replaying the gory picture in my head.

It was midnight, when we heard a loud crash against our front door. Kelly sat bolt upright in bed and began a banishment prayer that she had learned as a child from her grandmother:

In the name of the Father,
And the Son, and the Holy Spirit,
I banish you back from whence you came
Let evil be separated from me,
As far as the North is from South,
And the East is from the West. Amen.

I hurried over to see who or what was there, carefully peeking around the front door, expecting some crazed criminal or troublemaker, and saw nothing outside. But Kelly would not stop praying, and the very air in the room seemed charged with unseen energy. Slowly, after much time and many prayers, it lessened until there some feeling of peace, and we were able to go back to sleep.

The following day was even more surreal. I had stored a few things at a friend's house across town, and he also reported a loud noise in the room that these items were in. It was as if something heavy had hit the floor hard. But, upon racing in to see what had happened, he too had found nothing. Both of these events had occurred at the same time, in different places. I was the only common denominator.

We didn't know what to make of it all, so we ran away to Governor's Square, a popular mall in Tallahassee, as if bright and shiny shops filled with beautiful things could erase it all. We felt like Rod Serling in ***The Twilight Zone***. Now this was on a humid afternoon in Tallahassee, the sky threatening rain and the air filled with repressive heat. Such ordinary surroundings called for ordinary struggles- family, careers- the basic give and take of existence- not a struggle against dark powers and principalities. But for the spiritual storm, the Chick-Fil-A, our favorite restaurant, was quiet as we sat eating chicken nuggets, trying to make sense of these two seemingly random events.

I gazed absentmindedly into the back of the restaurant, and at first, my eyes kind of slid over what I was seeing. Then, realization washed over me. Silently standing there, watching our every move was a black woman in a gray dress with a blue kerchief on her head.

"Are they holding a Civil War reenactment or something?" I wondered aloud.

"Not that I'm aware of. What are you looking at?"

"A woman dressed in a gray dress with a blue kerchief. Looks like she came straight out of **Gone with the Wind**.*"*

Kelly looked back into what she saw was an empty dining area.

"I don't see anybody."

"Well, she's there." I looked back at her, and our eyes met. *"I can't believe that you don't see her."*

Then, Kelly went suddenly rigid, as if she understood what was going on. Her voice had a note of wonder, when she said, *"You're looking at the Bell Witch. Show respect."*

It was hard to breathe, and the floor felt as though it was going to give away beneath me. She calmly walked over to the table, and placed her hand on mine. I felt suddenly cold and shivered. Then, she spoke to me, probably the first words uttered to a living soul in over a century.

"Don't you ever hurt my baby."

As fantastical as it may seem, this ghost can often speak, and even hostile accounts of her have her speaking. But to hear such a thing is more than a little disconcerting. You, the reader, must understand that this ghost isn't "ye olde psychic recording" that is seen but not interacted with. Kate is a genuine entity with a mind and direction of her own. She is not limited like other spirits. To hear her speak is like someone leaning in and whispering in your ear. And there is always the feeling of warmth and protection when I encounter her.

Occasionally, I will also smell a deep, woodsy kind of scent-like you'd find in the heart of a forest. (From time to time, I've smelled a flowery odor when Kelly's Nana is around. This is interesting because Kelly told me that her grandmother was known for beautiful flowers and was an excellent green thumb.)

But on this first time interacting with the ghost, I could only swallow hard, turned my head, look her in the eye, and answer with all the nerve that I could muster (which wasn't much,)*"I'd never do that. I love her too much."*

Then, I couldn't help myself; I weakly added, *"Exactly how long has she been your baby?"*

"I sang that chile lullabies in her crib, a lifetime ago- when she could see me."

That was the beginning of the strangest evening in my life. No seances, spells, potions or incantations, not even EVP, infrared cameras, or temperature sensors- just simple communication- asking questions and getting answers.

I'm a lifelong scholar, so my fear was quickly eclipsed with curiosity. I was having an experience that many people would give the world to have. I suppose that it was weird for Kelly to watch her Mr. Wizard engage with the supernatural. After all, I had always prized reason, logic, math and science.

At one point, Kelly turned to us and whispered frantically, *"I get that the ghost is here. I get that you're having a real light bulb moment, but to coin a phrase from the movies: 'you're scaring the straights!!'"*

Looking around us, we did see a few people staring at me as if I were on loan from the asylum. But I was so excited that I couldn't help but continue the conversation. So, acting as though I were speaking to Kelly, I mumbled on.

At first, it was *"Are you really the Bell Witch?"*

"Yes."

"Who was Jesus of Nazareth?"

Kate smiled as if she had known that this test was coming. Christians have used it for centuries in discerning the true nature of spirits. And looking me in the eye, she calmly declared, ***"Jesus of Nazareth was born the Christ, the Son of the Living God."***

Her declaration is very important as no demon can willingly acknowledge Christ as the Son of God. Instead, they will often say that He was a great teacher or leader, but to declare Him "Lord" or "God" is against their rebellious nature. Now, I was seriously taken aback, so I continued: *"Why are you here?"*

"To guard you.

"From what?"

"What you woke up. Dante was right."

I cocked my head as if I'd not heard her correctly, "Dante? From the Divine Comedy?

"Tha's the man. Your replay of that movie's bloody scene was like an invite, and it decided to take ya up on it."

A fresh new wave of shock seemed to overwhelm me. I tried to sound casual when I asked, *"What's "it"?"*

"A demon."

"I summoned a demon?!"

"Yep."

"But it was all make believe, even in the movie."

"It don't matter. It's the images that you can't let go of. You dwell on 'em too much. That critter's a pit fiend. It loves bloodshed. You can't watch anymore movies like that. It's too dangerous."

The following week also felt as though it were a blur. The ghost refused to leave us- emphasizing that the danger was far from over.

"It still wants to come over. You need to stay away from violent thoughts and anger of any kind. Mark you house and pray."

Pray? All these statements and actions were not those of a malevolent being. Demons don't tell the spiritually oppressed to pray to God for deliverance. And they absolutely refuse to acknowledge Jesus as the Son of God. It was obvious that this ghost had truly been vilified.

Mark the house? Feeling a bit uncomfortable about asking for a large amount of Holy Water from the local Catholic Church, Kelly took a 5 qt. Dutch oven, filled it with tap water, and added a large quantity of salt, and lifting it up to the ceiling, called down the presence of the Holy Spirit as best she could.

We walked around our little duplex, sprinkling the ground and our car, and marking each window and door with the cross and the Alpha and Omega symbols. Then, we did the interior of the apartment- all of this accompanied by Kelly's banishment prayer. And no matter how much my mind wanted to stray to the bloody scene in the movie, it couldn't. Kate stayed very close. I'm not really sure how she did it, but she would change the images in my head like you flip a channel on a TV.

Over the next seven days, tempers flared, and there was a terrible feeling of anger and frustration bristling in the air. It was as if the creature that I had attracted was running out of time to act- looking for any way to override the spiritual protection that we had put in place. The pressure was so great that we fled to my parent's home in Monticello, offering to house sit, anything to get away from it. But at the end of the seventh day, the invisible tension broke, and I heard a distant and painful wail of something that had never been human. The door had been shut for good- sealed against its entry. But the ghost remained and our adventures were just starting.

Money from Empty Wallets

Tim's Memories

Katya had grown fond of me. She certainly liked the respect we gave her. My accidental brush with the super-natural world had left me with "spirit eyes," and she found that she could communicate with me on the easiest level- just like living human beings talk with one another, which is extremely rare for a ghost. While Kelly could sense Kate, she'd long lost the ability to see her. Babies and small children will see what teens and adults cannot.

I once asked her why Kelly could no longer see her. Kate smiled, chuckled and answered, ***"Inside, she's too much like me. It's like takin' two pictures of people who look alike, putting 'em on top of each other, then tryin' to pull 'em apart. Part of me would be with her and part of her would stay with me. It's just too dangerous for both of us. But you're diff'rent enough for us to talk."***

Being given spirit eyes can be very strange at times. Other ghosts usually know that you see them and will seek you out. Once on our birthday, we went up to see the outdoor drama, ***"Horn in the West,"*** which is shown nightly during the spring and summer months in Boone, NC. This musical drama takes place at the early part of the Revolutionary War and boasts canon, musket fire and one particular historical building- a cabin. As I toured it, I remember seeing people puttering around inside, wearing period garb. I looked over at my wife and muttered, *"Some of these people haven't left their home yet."*

On our 10th Anniversary Renewal of Vows, my wife's best friend's mother came up to me talking very animatedly about the beauty of the ceremony. She had died around 9 yrs earlier. I had to gently remind her that she was dead, that we were entertaining guests, and that I couldn't talk at that time.

At least twice, Katya has pulled the veil completely away from my eyes and allowed me to see the spiritual realm. Some things defy any mortal's description. It would be like describing a rainbow to a person blind since birth. Once I remember seeing a demon in its most natural form. It was nothing like Hollywood pictures demons to be. Think of beings so incredibly beautiful that you can barely stand to gaze at them, but with deadened eyes as if rotting from the inside out.

If we were to pull the veil away from mortal eyes, what we would see would be terrifying. The air is literally teeming with spirits, angels and demons, and there is a spiritual war with human souls as the prize. Every time I become even a little complacent, I remember what I saw. Often what we see and experience as a haunting is the most vocal and active of spiritual entities.

But on a humorous note, I once saw what appeared to be a piece of paper dancing on the wind. Laughingly, the ghost showed me what was really going on. Apparently, a group of goblin-like creatures were having something akin to a soccer match.

I'd like to share the revelation that this ghost senses emotion in a different way than living humans. For Kate, love is like a warm blanket or a mug of hot chocolate. But anger and hatred feel like hearing fingernails scratching a blackboard. Emotional responses have a sensory feeling to them like hearing, touch, and smell. I think that Katya was drawn to the love that she felt was between Kelly and me. It not only boasted attraction but friendship and mutual respect. (After over 25 years, it's still that way.)

I've always found that most people are either lucky in love or money- but rarely both. True to that statement, our biggest problem lay in paying the bills. But we would always put everything we made together, pay the bills, and then spend what was left as a couple. There was never a moment of his versus hers or mine versus yours. We knew sharing well.

Even so, things were often tight, and one set of my friends were too used to using me as their own personal piggy bank and unpaid laborer. I speak of Miri and Cameron, who lived next door. These 60's rejects had tried to break us up when it became clear that we were engaged and that the free money and labor were not going to continue. When that failed, Miri and Cameron became determined to bully me to get occasional funding. I've always been generous, and have always had trouble saying "no" to people. Kelly has no such problem, especially when dealing with declared enemies.

One day near our first Christmas, Miri stood at the apartment door, yelling for me to come out and face her. Kelly firmly told her that I didn't want to talk to her. (She was trying to keep a straight face at the time because I was sheepishly peaking out from the door of another room, shaking my head.)

No, we didn't have extra funds; we barely had enough for ourselves. Realizing she wasn't about to win, Miri stormed off and slammed her door. Kelly and I hoped that it was all over and breathed a little easier. After an untroubled night's sleep and an early breakfast, I locked up to go to work as Kelly drifted back to sleep, cuddling with our new kitten, Sugar, a calico with cinnamon and gray markings.

A few hours later, in early morning dreams, Kelly heard a gasp and our front door slamming. Waking with a start, Kelly climbed out of bed and hurried into living room. It had seemed so real, but nothing looked out of place, so she groggily went back to sleep. That evening, we discovered an unlocked front door and $40 dollars missing from our bedroom bureau. Then, we remembered that Miri had had a key to the apartment, and we had never changed the locks.

It was pretty obvious what had happened, but we had no evidence of a break-in. As a deterrent, we brought in Maggie, my "littermate" from my parents' home in Monticello, who was half-Pit Bull, half-German Shepherd, and all muscle. It worked; it was very easy to gain entrance, but staring down at a mouth full of sharp teeth probably had an unnerving effect. I remember once we had had an altercation with the landlord, and he had made the mistake of touching the door of the apartment. Maggie jumped on and dug her claws into the screen, which was jarred loose from the door frame. Kelly quickly grabbed the collar to keep our dog from harming the foolish man.

As for our break-in, the police refused to be bothered over something that was next to impossible to prove. Even worse was the fact that that was our last $40 until we had another payday in two weeks. It was our gas, laundry, and grocery money, and we didn't know what to do.

Now, I worked at a local gas station and had managed to collect Canadian coins. So, in desperation, we were doing our laundry using this tiny bit of money that wasn't even US coins. It was enough to handle a few loads, but gas and groceries were still a problem. We sat debating what to do. Get money from my parents? Ugh! A loan from another friend? Most of our friends were just as penniless as we were.

The dryer stopped, and on top of the clothes, we found two crisp, brand new twenty dollar bills. It was obvious that the bills had not been washed. Washed money is wrinkled and never flat and crisp. These two beauties had never been folded. Comparing their serial numbers, we noted that they had been printed side by side in the same printing house.

We were able to put gas in the car and buy much needed food for the house. Then, I seemed to feel Katya's presence, and crooking my head, asked aloud, *"Was that you, Kate?"*

All I heard in response was a soft tinkling laughter, like wind chimes. I grinned at Kelly and said, *"She's laughing."*

Incidents like this became common place. Whenever times got really tight, we'd find tens and twenties tucked in previously empty shirts and pants' pockets. On many occasions, this was comical. One time, I remember giving Kelly my last dollar, hanging my shirt over a chair, then finding another dollar in that pocket a few minutes later.

Kelly would ask me if I had any money. Was I sure we had nothing left? I'd sometimes hand her my wallet and declare exasperatedly, *"Whatever's in there is yours!"*

Folks, when a man hands you his wallet and says that sentence, you can bet that it's empty. Well, Katya has left as much as $79.00 in my wallet at one time. Kelly giggled at my pained expression as she pocketed it for much needed food, laundry and gas. Once we needed coins for the laundry, and we managed find a roll of quarters for the machines in a place where there hadn't been any money five minutes earlier.

Over the years, Kate would continue this patronage. It was around the holidays one year that we took pity on stranded travelers- giving money when we ourselves worried about making the bills. As we came home, I heard her whisper, ***"Go and look in your lunchbox."*** That evening, we found close to a hundred dollars in a previously empty lunchbox- a place where I didn't usually store money.

Even into our second decade together, there would be hard times where money was very scarce. In 2006, my left hand was crushed at work, and we were twisting in the financial wind-waiting on an elusive settlement that promised us release. The stress was so bad that Kelly had a second miscarriage of a much awaited and wanted child. (It's sad when those who dream of being parents are denied that honor.) Then in December of 2008, near Christmas, Kelly almost died from bacterial pneumonia, spending 2 weeks in ICU, 10 days of which were on a ventilator, then another 3 weeks learning how to walk, stand, and use her hands again. After being released, she still needed another month to get her strength and balance back. It was a terrible time in our lives, and we were barely making ends meet, despite help from many friends and relatives. Every once and a while, a mysterious amount of money would materialize in an unexpected spot.

Being pretty honest people, we would sometimes ask, "*Where do you get this money?*"

I'd hear a chuckle and the answer, ***"From those who don't deserve it, won't miss it, and can't use it!"***

"What? Criminals?"

"Maybe."

"So, some drug dealer is missing part of his stash."

"Could be." And that was all she would ever really say.

When we went to see Disney's ***The Princess and the Frog*** at our local $2 Cinema, we planned to just pay admission, but Kate thought otherwise. We found an extra $5.00 for popcorn and drinks.

Katya and Cable TV

Tim's Memories

It's interesting to note that this ghost story is not about the peculiar goings on in a home, business, piece of land, etc. This is about being haunted as a person. So, Kelly and I could move to Timbuktu, and Kate would follow us. That said, there are a number of strange incidents that did and still do occur at home. Katya has messed with clocks and sent our animals running in every direction. I'm convinced that cats and dogs see what human eyes cannot and respond accordingly.

But when this spirit doesn't like what's on TV, you might just have trouble watching it. From time to time, there are segments on the Bell Witch done by this or that paranormal show. Katya invariably shows her aggravation by messing with the picture or sound quality. Hey, we're talking cable, where you generally don't get weird reception. It could be sunny and peaceful outside, but the TV will fuzz up or be difficult to hear for that one part of the show.

One of my more humorous experiences involved watching a segment on the Bell Witch where the picture started to slowly rotate until it was on its side. Kelly had gone to work, and I was just relaxing at home. The TV had started reviewing the accepted legend of the Bell Witch and slowly, without reason, the picture began to twist.

I should say that this is almost impossible to do as modern TVs do not operate like that. What the viewer is actually seeing is a point of light going across and down so fast that we see images rather than just that one point of light. A rotating picture just cannot happen because of the mechanics of how the image is actually seen.

In spite of this basic scientific fact, the image did move until it was on its side. Exasperated, I stared at the ceiling and called out, ***"I know that you think it's all lies, but let me watch it anyway. It's not going to turn me against you."*** A few minutes later, the picture began to move back to its regular position, and everything was normal by the time the next story had come on.

Another time, I made the mistake of saying something like that in front of a high school friend of my wife's, to which the woman fled the house- completely freaked out. This reinforced the painful lesson of addressing spirits out loud in front of strangers and people who could never understand. And most people cannot understand what's going on because they don't have spirit eyes and dismiss anything that cannot be observed or quantified by independent sources. My world, despite my love of science, logic, and reason, is not that comfortable.

The Lady in the Mirror

Kelly's Memories

I've mentioned that Katya is very fond of an old dresser which was inherited from my grandmother. It has a rich, reddish brown finish with a round mirror that has begun to warp with age. Most people don't know that glass is technically a highly viscous liquid which flows very slowly. This is why antique glass (especially window panes and mirrors) tends to have a "melted" look.

As much as I would like to keep it out, its age, along with a nasty crack down the front, has rendered it too fragile for use anymore. So, the dresser is currently being used as computer desk in our kitchen. It's a shame really, considering that mirror's history. Two people, on two different occasions saw Kate. They never met or compared notes.

During my time in Florida (18 mos), we managed to acquire a temporary roommate, named Sam. In our first apartment, we found that the air conditioner worked better in the living room. So, we had begun sleeping on this futon-like bed that I had found at a local department store. That left the back bedroom free. So, we didn't mind it when he moved in. As he was putting his things away, he came out of our bedroom, in a bemused state. Looking at both us, he asked, ***"Who's the lady in the mirror?"***

Now, we hadn't said a word about a ghost. We glanced at each other and queried back, ***"What lady in what mirror?"***

"In that old dresser mirror, I thought that I saw a black lady. She looked like she had a blue bandana on her head."

"Did she say anything to you?"

"Not a word. She was gone before I could react."

Now, we were impressed! For the first time, an outsider saw this spirit, and he wouldn't be the only one.

Martin is an old friend with a taste for cowboy boots and hats and a weakness for Asian women and silky, long black hair. Kind of odd, considering he's African-American. Intelligent and wisecracking, this guy earned the moniker, "Sheriff" from the late British actor, Jon Pertwee, at a convention.

After relocating back to Salisbury, my father had found us another shoebox apartment, and Martin had begun to hang out with us a lot- opting to sleep in the living room. This was because his grandmother had been placed in a nursing home as she could no longer care for her house. Having been through such an experience myself, I knew that he'd be depressed from the whole ordeal and really not want to stay at his grandma's place. So, he stayed with us on a regular basis. One day, he came out into the kitchen from the bathroom, a little dumbfounded.

"Kelly, I swear that I've just saw this woman in your mirror!"

"What?"

"It was just a head, but she looked like she was black."

We were no longer easily stunned, but asked back, ***"What was she wearing?"***

"A blue scarf on her head. Who was that?"

"Just Kate, the family ghost."

Apparently Kate also liked Martin, but in a different way. At another time, he had been in the living room while I was busy cleaning elsewhere. Martin called out, ***"Kelly, did you kiss me?"***

I cocked my head and said, ***"No, why do you ask?"***

"It felt as though someone gave me a kiss on the cheek."

I told Martin that I had been nowhere near him at the time when Tim laughingly piped up and said, ***"I think I hear her giggling like a school girl. Hey, Martin, she LIKES you!"***

Those events took place in 1987 and 1989. In 1996, Tim and I were renting a cottage in the city. It was a charming little place that had French doors between the living room and the kitchen/dining room.

One evening, we were having a dinner party. (I love to cook for my friends.) And a fellow classmate was hanging out, just socializing, when he glanced over at the glass. Looking back at us, he said, ***"I could've sworn that I just saw a black lady reflected in a pane of glass in your doors there."***

We smiled at each other and back at him.

"What'd she look like?"

"Black lady. She was wearing one of those old fashioned starched white maid's caps, and I saw the collar of a black dress."

We were surprised that Kate wasn't wearing her regular outfit, her customary blue and gray apparel, but this time she had elected to wear something else. Then, we remembered that we were having a dinner. Perhaps, she wanted to look her best.

Katya Goes To Work

Kelly's Memories

Most of our experiences of Katya in the workplace speak mainly of a protective, occasionally amusing influence. But every so often, she'd get a little testy more out of frustration than anything else.

I've worked for years for Subway as a crew leader on weekends at night. In addition to the freshly baked breads, veggies, chips, and cookies, I occasionally serve up a healthy dose of history, culture, and ghost stories- particularly on warm summer evenings when traffic is low.

Late one night, I was telling about my family ghost to a co-worker, Mark, who felt that all ghosts were nothing but demons in disguise. This is the typical refrain of many Protestant Fundamentalists who want to classify every mystery out there.

I began to point out various scripture passages detailing the existence of spirits (as discussed earlier) to which Mark didn't have much to say. This was particularly problematic when I began speaking of biblical references to spirits, including that of Samuel, the prophet. It was a spirited debate which ended rather abruptly when my purse, which was large and filled with every kind of item imaginable, fell down from the top shelf, spilling its contents all over the prep table. As you read this book, you will find that this ghost doesn't like to be vilified in any way. Katya certainly showed her displeasure that evening.

Another time, I was busy doing the usual cleaning and straightening, and I was looking out over the sandwich board, when I saw the mayonnaise bottle, which I had just placed in the center of the board a few minutes earlier, go sailing off, as if an invisible hand had hit it hard. Nobody had been around it, and there was no breeze in the room. Like so many times before, I looked up at the ceiling and called out quietly, "***Okay, Kate, I know you're there. Could you ease up a bit, please?***"

The room quieted, as if whatever was there was content to be acknowledged. I share my ghost story with many people. I believe that this is one of my assignments in life. One young mother, Shari, was totally fascinated and declared that she wanted to see Katya. Fearing that getting her wish might be more than she could handle, I cautioned her, "***Don't say that! She might take you up on it!***"

As we didn't work together for a week or so, I forgot about the whole thing. The next time we were in the store, Shari excitedly told me that the spirit had apparently followed her home. Her 2-year-old toddler kept trying to feed cookies to a person she called ***"Mama Kate."*** And a visiting friend refused to stay in the living room, declaring that there was a presence there.

Katya Goes Bowling

Tim's Memories

The most colorful episode I had with Kate at work happened when I was working as a mechanic at our local bowling alley. Rick, a guy at the front desk, seemed more than a little tense one evening, and calling me over, he whispered, ***"By the way, did you know that you're haunted?"***

I couldn't help but smile. What had Kate been up to? I answered, ***"Yeah, I know. What's she look like?"***

He hesitated. ***"She's a black woman in a gray dress and a blue kerchief."***

"That's Kate. What's she been doing?"

"Mostly following you around every time you come up. Otherwise, she just stares at me. She's been watching me for over two hours!"

Rick went on to say that he knew she was a ghost because not only was her style of dress out of place, but she seemed transparent enough to see other customers milling about behind her. Rick was sensitive to the spectral world, but this was the first time he had actually seen a ghost.

And stranger still was the fact that Kate was interacting with him. This was definitely not some psychic recording or a being caught in an endless loop. Again, she displayed intelligence and an awareness of her surroundings.

I couldn't have been more pleased. Not only had someone else seen this specter, but they had witnessed her for a prolonged period of time. This was huge, and I couldn't wait to tell Kelly when I got home.

"Ockham's Razor"

Kelly Finishes the Tale

William of Ockham was an English scholar and Franciscan friar, specializing in philosophy, logic, physics and theology, who lived from 1287-1347. Reported to have been born in Ockham, a village in Surrey, he is the creator of the concept known as "Ockham's Razor." Pop culture often uses this in an abbreviated form, "the simplest explanation," but the actual statement is: "among competing hypotheses (educated guesses) the one that requires the fewest assumptions is to be preferred. In other words, "the simplest explanation that fits the facts and requires the fewest assumptions is preferred."

Whenever I speak of this legend that my father, a man close to his faith, gave me, it seems to resonate with a truth that other explanations of the Bell Witch phenomenon do not have. It makes sense whereas other theories seem to logically lack in some way.

Many people have noticed that I seem guarded by something, a protective presence. Maybe it's that I am a truly kindred soul when it comes to this ghost. It's difficult to reconcile the historical accounts of her with the description and actions that we've witnessed over the years. But they do coincide with our family legend. It is possible that this legend was circulated among slaves and less prominent members of the Adams community, and this is how my father may have received it, as he was a sharecropper's son.

I do believe that Betsy Bell may have buried the details documenting this slave's existence. Historians record that John Bell owned slaves; that much is certain. Think about how easy it would have been to erase written references of Kate, if any existed in the first place. Generally speaking, there was little documentation regarding the lives of slaves, particularly those born into slavery and never traded or sold like a dower slave, which is what our legend has always asserted. Betsy, from all accounts, loved her father. She probably was a "Daddy's Girl." I'm not saying that she was an evil person; it's possible that she was simply trying to protect her father and the family name.

I do not blame or harbor any resentment towards the Bell descendents. I don't know them, and they are only sharing what historical accounts have led them to believe. My accounts are first-hand, not based upon what this or that venerable person wrote decades or even a century ago. Given the fact that Adams remains a small community, it is a distinct possibility that I may be connected to the Bells in some remote way.

The origin of the Bell Witch has been linked to a spurned lover, bad business deals, poltergeist activity, demonic activity, Native American spirituality, even incest between Betsy and John Bell. But these ideas make little sense. Murder, however, is an excellent reason to haunt a family, and removing traces of the crime would definitely incense and enrage the spirit of the murdered individual. Not only has the individual been stripped of human freedom, dignity and life, but their very existence has been wiped away as if they never were in the first place. Here's what we know firsthand:

This specter gets upset when we watch segments on the Bell Witch. That's odd behavior for a spirit not unassociated with the legend or the Bell Witch. Could she be another spirit of another slave from the distant past in my mother's family? I teethed on legends and lore from my maternal grandmother's knee, and to my knowledge, none of my mother's people owned slaves. They considered slavery to be offensive. Nana spoke of how my great grandfather would get the doctor when any of his sharecroppers were ill, many of which were black and Amerind. Where, in a family with Quaker leanings, would Kate have come from?

Katya has generously left funds when we needed it, even warned us when we were in spiritual danger. She begged us to pray to the Trinity and mark our house. That's a severe conflict of interest and really strange behavior for a demon. Historical accounts speak of the spirit attending church, and even record her saying the words, "Lord Jesus." A demon cannot do that, will not ever utter those words. Under exorcisms and extreme duress, demons have called Jesus by other titles, but to say, "Lord Jesus" is like acid in their mouths and tantamount to defeat. Katya's declaration to my husband proves that she cannot be a demon, for she called Jesus, "Lord" and declared Him the Son of the Living God. (She can't be angel either, because she is still a prankster after all these years, causing merry mischief with our clocks, TVs, house guests and pets.)

A spurned lover of John Bell would not save the life of her rival, his wife. If anything, Lucy Bell would have been the biggest target aside from John. But the ghost's devotion to this woman definitely points to a loving relationship in life, as is documented in even in hostile accounts. Remember, Katya was treated with great respect and affection by Mrs. Bell in the legend that I grew up with. They were very close, which caused John Bell to seek to get rid of her or at least subdue her in some way so that he could retain his authority in the home, which he felt was being undermined.

Native spirituality doesn't fit either, though the "Bell Witch Cave" is situated on ancient burial ground. While there are many strange incidents associated with the Cave, Lucy Bell should have been targeted as well as the rest of the family. Most of the incidents recorded about this area deal with animistic manifestations like what you would find at a prehistoric site. Animism was the principal religion of prehistoric man, and the Amerind culture and religion remains richly woven in animistic concepts and rituals. Having visited and explored the Cave myself, there was the impression of entering a sacred site, marked by grief and other strong emotions.

Given my Amerind heritage, I was deeply respectful, but felt absolutely nothing that coincided with what I knew of our ghost. My husband who is very sensitive to her presence felt nothing of her there. The Bell Witch made Adams famous, and there is a tendency to put her title on anything and everything that is unexplained in this village. Obviously, there are other spirits and entities at work here in addition to Katya, but Amerind spirituality does not truly fit with Katya's legend in any way, given her declarations to and about Christ, both in our legend and in hostile accounts.

I won't dignify the idea of angst and incest causing the Bell Witch phenomenon. There are no historical accounts or personal observations from us supporting such a thing. This theory is nothing more than Hollywood's overactive imagination and complete lack of common sense. The film, ***American Haunting*** deeply insulted everyone's intelligence and demeaned any writer who has tried to be faithful to the facts.

I suppose that we could conclude that my husband is nuts or that he's lying; however, he remains a very rational, logical person in other regards, and twenty-six years is a long time to keep up the “dog and pony show.” Even stranger, is how he could've managed to get other witnesses to describe the same thing without being coached. That would be an awfully big conspiracy for no purpose other than to fool and confound his wife. And it would also be a cruel lie to perpetrate, and as my husband is very loving and kind, it would be against his character to do so.

I believe that the simplest explanation to this mystery is the best: John Bell was responsible for the horrific death of a household slave, and he paid for his actions with his life.

I believe that Betsy Bell never respected Katya in life, refused to obey her in death, and when she tried to marry Joshua Gardner, they both paid a heavy price for their folly. As a result, I also believe that Betsy further maligned this ghost by dehumanizing her and removing any trace of who she really was.

I believe that this spirit overshadowed my father and then me because we knew the truth, knew who she really was, and shared that legend with as many people as possible. Katya has harmed neither my father nor me nor any of my family. She continues her role as a kind of guardian of our home, a place rooted in the Christian faith and family, though recently, her presence is not as notable anymore.

But just when we think that she’s gone, she makes herself known. When doing my final revision of this book, we were once again running low on funds to the point of rationing gasoline and groceries. We looked in a previously empty wallet to find over $20.00 accompanied by musically tinkling laughter, like wind chimes on a breeze. I knew Katya still had her eye on us and could not help but smile and be grateful.

When sharing our version of the legend, many people have commented that they had heard of this version before. My personal theory is that there were two versions of this legend, the most popular version and a lesser known story circulated, by slaves, sharecroppers, and the poor of Adams. The one thing that seems to be a common refrain when people hear our version is that our legend makes more sense than the "party line."

One parting thought: Katya once told my husband that there is something that belongs to me, her heir, in Adams, TN. It is meant for me, and I will know it when I see it. It may be a tangible trace of the slave that I know as Kate or Katya, whom the rest of the world calls "the Bell Witch."

The Feast of All Souls

As a Protestant Fundamentalist, I had always found disturbing gaps in my spirituality, especially with regard to the realm of ghosts. Believing that there were just angels and demons at work didn't make a lot of sense. I concluded that those with that simplistic view were unacquainted with the nuances of a larger and more complex universe.

Martin Luther and other reformers embraced the Tanak, rather than the Septuagint for the basis of the Old Testament to eliminate the scriptural basis behind prayer for the dead. The problem is that the Protestant Bible (KJV 1611) remains riddled with passages alluding to a middle state of cleansing.

Even more powerful is the fact that Jesus never rebuked this belief, which was a big part of the Jewish faith, and the state of one's eternal soul is of paramount importance to both the Jewish and Christian faiths. If prayer for the dead were a heretical teaching, it is certain that Christ would have directly addressed the matter and clearly defined it as being so.

We still witness traces such as the "RIP" on tombstones (which stands for *"Requiescat in Pacem"* an implied prayer for the dead) and hear old folk, saying the words, *"God rest his/her soul,"* another prayer for the dead because there is an implied "may" in those words.

Protestant ministers will often say things like, *"Lord, please accept your servant..."* at funerals. But, if there's only heaven and hell, then why do that? Pray for the family, the community, etc because the person in question has gone on.

And so, as a Catholic Christian, I found it easy to believe in Purgatory. Every November 2nd, masses are held for the repose of those souls imprisoned there, some who are recently passed into eternity, others long dead. Nana was right to believe that our job is to help make the spiritual realm a more peaceful one. We must acknowledge the suffering dead and seek their release from torment.

This book was specifically written to do just that, to speak honestly of a trapped spirit, robbed of human dignity in both life and in death, in the hope that she may rest a little easier. It is doubtful that those who've written and researched the Bell Witch have any real experience of the ghost herself. I have shared 38 years of memories of a ghost who is a kind of spiritual grandmother, watching over me from my cradle. Katya is anything but the hellish tormentor she has been portrayed to be.

And so I leave you now, with my prayer for Katya's soul. If you wish, you may join me:

Katya's Song

In the Name of the Father, Son, and Holy Spirit,
Blessed Trinity, hear my cry.

To the spirit, who has guarded me from birth:
Beloved protectress, denied freedom in life,
I release you.

Defamed and maligned in death,
I, your voice, the singer of your song,
Restore your humanity.

Entrusting you to Eternal Mercy,
I knock on Heaven's Door, and beg your entrance to Paradise.
I implore the Lord Jesus Christ, King of the Universe,
To lovingly embrace you, receive you into his arms

So, that you may sit with angels and saints,
Martyrs and virgins,
And whisper in Our Lady's ear,
The smallest plea for her prayers,
For your child, still laboring, still fighting,
Still running the race.

So, that one day I will gaze upon you,
And we will share the Eternal Banquet,
The Marriage Feast,
And laugh and dream together,
At the end of time.
Amen.

Principal Writer- Kelly Stuard-Will
Associate Writer– Timothy M. Will

Chief Editor- Timothy M. Will

Formatting Editor- JR Tyner

Painting/Graphics- Kelly Stuard-Will,

Timothy M. Will and JR Tyner

 and is also dedicated to Gale Brewer, Amy L. Moorhead, Nancy M. Williams and all who still dream and believe.

References

Beliefnet, “Prayer for the Dead” <http://www.beliefnet.com/boards/message_list.asp?pageID=2&discussionID=219859>.

Doublass, Robert Sydney. "History of Southeast Missouri," 1992, pp. 32–45. Retrieved on 2013-05-29.

Henson, Timothy R. *The Black Patch Bells: The Story of John & Lucy Bell. 2003*

Ingram, MV. *Authenticated History of the Bell Witch and other Stories of the World's Greatest Unexplained Phenomenon.*

Pioneer Press. Union city, Tennessee, 2000.

Spade, Paul Vincent. "William of Ockham." *Stanford Encyclopedia of Philosophy*. Stanford University, 2002. Retrieved on 2013-05-27 from http:// plato.stanford.edu/entries/ockham/

Stuard-Will, Kelly. *A Faraway Ancient Country*, Karitas Publishing, 2004.

www.ingramcontent.com/pod-product-compliance
Ingram Content Group UK Ltd.
Pitfield, Milton Keynes, MK11 3LW, UK
UKHW041918190726
13854UKWH00003B/1317